KARATE

KARATE
Larry Dane Brimner

A First Book
FRANKLIN WATTS
New York/London/Toronto/Sydney/1988

All photographs (including the cover) are courtesy of the author

Library of Congress Cataloging-in-Publication Data

Brimner, Larry Dane.
Karate.

(A First book)
Bibliography: p.
Includes index.
Summary: Surveys the history of karate and
different karate styles and provides instructions
on basic moves, how to advance in the sport, and
how to get started in competitions.
1. Karate—Juvenile literature. [1. Karate]
I. Title. II. Series.
GV1114.3.B75 1988   796.8'153   87-25341
ISBN 0-531-10480-X

Contents

To
Frank Sloan,
editor and friend

For freely offering their time and knowledge,
the author wishes to thank Brian D. Manna
of the United Martial Arts Federation and
Minobu Miki of the Japan Sports Center.

1
The Past

Karate is the Asian method of self-defense, using principally the hands and feet to defend one's self. The exact origin of karate is a mystery. It is known to have existed thousands of years ago in India. There, according to folklore, weaponless warriors single-handedly defended themselves on the battlefield. Ancient Indian art and temple sculptures depict warriors in stances surprisingly similar to those of today's karate.

More is known about the spread of karate into China. In A.D. 500, a Buddhist monk named Bodhidharma made a spiritual journey across his native India and into neighboring China. It was his purpose to spread knowledge, but his journey was plagued by frequent attacks of armed robbers.

Dharma, as Bodhidharma was called, was a religious man and carried no weapons. The only defense he had was his empty hands and a knowledge of a martial-art form that made it possible for him repeatedly to fend off his attackers.

When Dharma arrived at the Shaolin-Szu monastery in China, he demonstrated the techniques he had used to defend himself. The monks were so impressed that they asked Dharma to remain at Shaolin-Szu to teach them these skills. His fighting technique

was soon accepted as part of the formal training activity at the monastery, not only because of its obvious benefit in self-defense, but also because the intense concentration required of students was seen as an aid in enlightening the mind. In time, the Shaolin-Szu monks gained the reputation of being the foremost champions of the technique in China.

Others became interested in the skill, too. China and the Far East had long been an area of warring lords who fought for power and riches. Once an area had been conquered, the victors took what they pleased from those unable to defend themselves. And since peasants were forbidden to possess weapons, some trained in the empty-handed fighting technique so that they might have a way to protect their property. The secret training led to the development of local styles, but they all retained the basic concepts of mental concentration and swift, powerful action.

Years later, the idea of an unarmed militia was used in Okinawa, an independent island at that time. Because of its strategic location, Okinawa had suffered many invasions. During one such invasion, by Japan, all weapons were confiscated, but the Okinawans planned to retaliate anyway.

Before the plan was put into action, the Japanese learned of the scheme. Surprisingly, they did not react with hostility; they were curious. What was this defensive skill that the Okinawans possessed? Why did they have such complete faith in its ability to outwit an obviously stronger foe?

The Japanese invaders asked for demonstrations of this form of defense, and the Okinawans presented their best fighter,

Karate is principally a weaponless self-defense technique. An inside block is demonstrated.

Gichin Funakoshi, to show his power. Funakoshi was so successful at defending himself that he received an invitation to Japan's Imperial Palace in 1922 to demonstrate the "new" martial art, which the Japanese dubbed "karate"—from the Japanese *kara* (empty) and *te* (hand).

Once in Japan, Funakoshi was greeted by skeptics. At 5 feet 1 inch tall (155 cm), he was thought to be no match for the large and powerful sumo wrestlers. Yet, repeatedly, he brought his opponents to the mat, and his image changed.

Funakoshi soon attracted a large following and established a *dojo* (school). His students called the school *shotokan,* which means house of willow. *Shoto,* or willow tree, was Funakoshi's nickname, because his limber body enabled him to flex like that tree. He put off his return to Okinawa and continued teaching in Japan until his death in 1957 at the age of eighty-eight. Today, Funakoshi is remembered as the father of modern karate.

Karate remained an oriental skill until after World War II, when returning American military men brought information about the martial art home with them. By the late 1950s, karate had developed a strong enough following in the United States to warrant a national tournament schedule.

In the two decades that followed, movies featuring Chuck Norris and the late Bruce Lee captured the attention of many, and fans inspired by their high-action stunts enrolled in training schools to develop their own skills. More recently, movies like *The Karate Kid*, *Karate Kid II*, and *Steele Justice*, and television programs like *Sidekicks* have caught the imagination of a new generation of *karateka* (student). Today, karate schools are commonplace in communities throughout the United States and in most parts of the world.

2
Why Study Karate?

The art of karate is practiced in over 120 countries throughout the world. People study karate for a variety of reasons. The World Union of Karate Organizations (WUKO), which sponsors world-wide championship competition, reports that its membership includes more than 100 nations and is growing. Just what is karate's attraction?

On a very basic level, karate is one of the most simplified of sports. Anybody can enjoy it, anytime, anywhere. No special equipment is necessary. But it is a sport to be taken seriously, under the supervision of a trained adult.

In an age when more and more people are concerned about their physical fitness, karate offers a way to exercise the *whole* body. Its range of movement provides training and development for all the muscles of the body. The concentration required to complete the various techniques successfully forces the mind to focus.

Many people feel that we are living in violent times and that the chances of becoming a victim of crime increase each day. Karate always has been and continues to be a means of self-defense. Every body gesture of karate is designed for combat.

*A sport practiced by all ages, karate
study often begins early in life.*

This is why most urban police departments require their recruits to become familiar with karate techniques. It is also why more and more men and women of all ages are choosing karate as a sport. Not only does karate increase their self-confidence, but it also makes them less vulnerable.

Karate stresses self-discipline, self-control, humility, and respect for others. Young people who study karate generally do better in school, often scoring higher on standard achievement tests. And adults who regularly train in karate usually manage the stresses of contemporary living more successfully than those who have no karate background.

Consider what karate offers. If you want to perform better in school, to show greater confidence, or to move with more poise and grace, it's a natural sport for you to study.

3
Karate Styles

A person who wishes to enroll in a karate school today is faced with a variety of styles—*tang soo do, tae-kwon do,* and *shoto-kan,* to name but a few. In part, the difference in styles is a result of karate's history of secret training. But a difference in basic philosophy is also reflected in the various styles.

Tang soo do is a complete martial art dating back to the original karate of China and India. Incorporating weaponry, hand-to-hand combat, and philosophy, tang soo do stresses kicks, which use legs and feet, over punches, which use arms and hands, about two-thirds of the time. The philosophy is that by frequently relying on kicks, the heart and head are kept farther from danger. In Korea, tang soo do was the prevalent form of martial art until a

Tang soo do karate incorporates the use of weaponry. Two versions of staff fighting are shown.

nationalistic movement swept the nation in the early 1950s. Then, the Korean leaders wanted something that would be identified solely with their country, and the sport of tae-kwon do was the result.

Tae-kwon do is now also called Korean karate. Developed by incorporating the techniques of tae kyun, an ancient form of foot fighting, Chinese kung fu (the Chinese version of karate), and karate, tae-kwon do was used by the military. It gained widespread publicity during the Vietnam War, where it was well-known as a brutal combat technique that frequently employed disabling kicks to the head. Today, tae-kwon do is widely practiced and respected as one of the strongest forms of self-defense known.

Shotokan is the style of karate developed by Gichin Funakoshi and is still a popular style today. There are at least twenty to twenty-five major shotokan associations in the United States alone. And each association seems to stress its own interpretation of technique and philosophy. Typically, however, shotokan karate stresses maximum power through swift and direct blows using the arms and hands as much as the legs and feet. It also relies on a series of *katas,* or dancelike movements, to teach self-defense in a variety of situations. It is believed that without Funakoshi's katas, shotokan karate would have become a forgotten martial art.

Though each style of karate claims to be the best, they all have something positive to offer. Karate, as it is practiced today, trains the student in discipline, concentration, and physical and cardiovascular fitness regardless of the style.

4
Karate Ranks

Tradition has always played an important role in karate. Original-ly, the beginning and advanced students were distinguished from the instructor by wearing white belts. Instructors, or karate mas-ters, wore black belts. The colors were symbolically important. It was felt that the white represented purity with no knowledge of technique. The instructors wore black, however, to symbolize a knowledge of karate that had been darkened with actual experi-ence.

Today, karate rank is still recognized by the color of the uni-form belt you wear. The standard belts, in order of expertise, are white, green, brown or red, and black. The additional colors were arbitrarily chosen, but some "experts" will tell you that the color green stands for a person whose knowledge of karate is awaken-ing. Brown or red represents a person whose knowledge has blossomed, and perhaps he has had to turn his knowledge into experience through actual, though limited, combat. Whether true or not, their symbolic significance makes for a good story.

Below the black belt, each level of achievement is called a *gup* or *kyu.* As your experience increases, your gup-level number decreases. That is, a fifth-gup green belt is better able to execute karate techniques than a sixth-gup green belt. Some schools give no ranking at the white-belt level. Others rank the white belt as ninth and tenth gups.

The black belt ranks are called *dan* (or degree). As you gain experience and expertise, you will be promoted from first dan to second dan, and so on.

In recent times, many schools have added other colors to their ranking systems. Yellow or orange represents a level between white and green. Purple or blue is sometimes chosen for the step between green and brown. The additional colors can encourage students who might think that advancing to a new gup isn't enough visible proof of achievement.

Before you can advance in rank, you are required to pass promotional examinations. Usually, these exams are held two to four times a year and are judged by high-ranking black belt instructors.

A promotional examination will customarily include specific katas, or forms—a series of dancelike movements consisting of blocks, strikes, kicks, and stances—which you are expected to know for each belt and for each rank within a belt. The higher your rank, the more katas you're expected to know.

It is typical for white- and green-belt katas to stress the basic stances, kicks, punches, and blocks. The higher-rank katas concentrate on proper breathing, muscular movement and control, power, flexibility, and grace.

5
Safety Equipment

In sport competition, karate strikes and kicks are performed with control. To score a point, it is more important to show that you have the ability to cause harm to your adversary if it becomes necessary. But all hits stop just short of connection.

As in any sport, however, karate carries with it a certain amount of risk. There are times when even a very skilled practitioner of karate fails to control a strike. Without proper body gear, injury is likely to result. This was the case at a recent competition, where two advanced students were competing in freestyle sparring. One of the contestants failed to stop her kick in time, and her foot made contact with her opponent's elbow, pushing the arm upward and causing the bone to snap at the shoulder joint. It is because of this potential for injury that most karate schools require students to purchase and practice with appropriate safety equipment.

At the very least, students should wear padded hand and foot gear when they begin sparring. Male students should always wear an athletic cup and supporter to protect the groin.

As you advance in rank and technique, some schools recommend a padded type of helmet that provides full head protection

and visibility. You can also select a rib guard to protect the mid-section of the body. Because shins and forearms are especially subject to contact, special guards are available to protect these areas.

A boxer wouldn't enter the ring without boxing gloves. Neither should a karate student enter into sparring or free-fighting without adequate protection.

When sparring, students should wear padded hand and foot gear.

6
Getting Started

Before any strenuous activity, a warm-up is suggested to loosen up your body. Slowly stretching your muscles creates enough body heat to prevent pulling, straining, or tearing.

A warm-up routine also allows you to demand the most of your muscles. Tense muscles do not perform as freely or with the same speed as relaxed ones. Performing lightning-quick moves and flying kicks requires limber and trained muscles, making a regular warm-up routine a vital part of being a karate master.

Experts suggest that your warm-up exercises be limited to a half hour every other day at first. Gradually, you can work up to a complete warm-up routine every day.

Several exercises are described here to get you started. More varied and extensive warm-ups and stretches are needed. For a more complete routine, ask your karate instructor.

NECK ROTATION

With your hands on your waist and your spine straight, slowly move your head in a circular motion, at first clockwise, then counterclockwise. Repeat this several times in each direction.

ARM ROTATION

Extend your arms out to your sides. Slowly rotate both arms in a small circle from front to back, gradually increasing the size of the circle. Repeat this in the opposite direction.

SHOULDER EXERCISE

Begin with your arms extended overhead and crossed. Keeping them stiff, slowly bring your arms straight down to the sides. As your arms become parallel to the body, press them backward to put pressure on your shoulder and chest muscles.

LEG STRETCH I

Keeping the spine straight, step forward with one leg and bend the knee over the toes. Extend the other leg as far back as possible, and lower the torso toward the floor. After holding this position for thirty seconds, switch legs and repeat.

LEG STRETCH II

Sit on the floor with your legs wide apart. Lean forward and grasp your right ankle or foot, lowering your head toward your right knee. Repeat and hold this position several times; then duplicate the exercise to the left.

PUSH-UPS

Lie stomach down on the floor. Keeping your back and legs straight, lift the body by pushing up with the arms, hands posi-

Leg Stretch I

Leg Stretch II requires loose muscles to extend fully.

tioned at the shoulders. Good for general body conditioning, push-ups can be done on the first two knuckles of the fist to strengthen the wrists, on the fingertips to strengthen the fingers, or, traditionally, with palms flat on the floor.

7
White Belt

At each rank, the karate student builds upon a solid foundation. If the foundation is weak or flawed, the finished structure will not be as strong as it could or should be. As you might guess, building a flawless foundation is not an easy task. It takes time, patience, concentration, and practice.

The karate school that moves its students too quickly into simulated combat (sparring) should be approached with caution. Regardless of the style or philosophy, karate basically remains a self-defense technique. As you advance in skill, your ability to act in your own defense improves. You'll gain more confidence and become able to anticipate an opponent's next move. However, each new skill must be built on previous skills or gaps will result, putting you at risk in a real life-threatening situation. Without the proper foundation, the techniques of defense practiced in karate will not be as accurate and smooth as necessary for *successful* hand-to-hand combat.

The time requirements may vary from school to school. It isn't unusual to spend three to four months practicing basic skills before advancing to primary one-step sparring. If the karate school you anticipate joining promises you a black belt in six months or freestyle sparring in four weeks, BEWARE!

Karate is composed of a system of stances, strikes (punches), kicks, and blocks. They should be done only when an instructor is present. You will be expected to learn a specific series of these before advancing to the next level or rank. The order in which these are taught varies from school to school and from instructor to instructor. What this book attempts to present is a realistic sampling of techniques that you may be introduced to at each rank. But your school may still approach it differently.

STANCE

Stance forms the foundation upon which all other techniques are built. The first stance learned in karate is the formal attention stance. It is used for bowing in and out of class, kata, and sparring matches. To take the stance, stand with the spine straight and erect, with your feet together. Your hands should be open at your sides.

The next stance learned at the white-belt level is the natural front stance. From this stance, you will be ready to move into any position, and almost all blocking, punching, and kicking techniques can be done from this position.

The feet should be spread shoulder-width apart, with the heels dug into the floor to "lock in" the position. The arms are held to the sides, slightly in front of the body, and the fists are clenched tightly.

After learning the natural stance, you'll be introduced to the front stance. Starting from the natural stance, step forward with either the right or left leg. Bend the forward knee over the toe.

The natural front stance

The rear leg is bent only slightly, and the thigh and calf muscles are locked in to gain stability. With both feet facing forward, your torso remains perpendicular to the ground.

The front stance is most widely used in practicing the basic techniques of blocking, punching, and kicking. It provides a balanced position and a forward motion when practicing drills. However, before you combine this stance with other techniques, practice it alone by stepping forward and backward until the movement becomes smooth and natural. The basic rule in moving the body is to shift the hips and then the legs in a smooth, gliding motion.

Balance is the key to the stances. When you balance a pencil on your finger, its balance point is close to the center of the pencil. Similarly, it is believed that the body's balance point—the *hara*, or *chung shim*—is just below the navel. To maintain stability, it is necessary to keep the balance point as close to the ground as possible. This is why so many of the stances assume a knees-bent position. A firm balance will give you the advantage over an untrained adversary.

STRIKE

The power generated in a karate strike is similar to that produced by a snapping whip; that is, the force from the whip should begin in the handle, travel the length of the whip, and be at its maximum power at the point of release. Similarly, the power of a karate strike must begin in the body and be at its fullest potential just at impact. How is this accomplished?

*Both feet face forward
in the front stance to
provide stability.*

While it is true that your muscles must be tight and tensed to increase power, tenseness reduces speed, and speed is the essence of karate. The trick is to throw a loose punch for speed and to tense up just before striking the target for a powerful impact. This technique is called "focus."

The first strike learned in karate is likely to be the thrust punch. Starting from the natural stance, your left fist, palm down, is extended straight out toward your opponent's solar plexus (the point just below the breastbone). Your right fist, palm up, is in the "chamber," a position just above your own waist, next to the lowest rib. As you draw back your left fist into its chamber, you thrust out your right fist, turning it in a corkscrew fashion so that the front two knuckles of the fist do the striking.

The lunge punch is the same as the thrust punch, but with the added benefit of forward motion. That is, at the same time you throw the punch, you step forward into the front stance. The striking fist and the forward leg should be on the same side, as this strike gains its power from the forward momentum.

Drawing its strength from the rotation of the hips, the reverse punch is the most commonly used strike in karate. It is said that one famous karate master could kill charging bulls with his powerful reverse punch.

Taken from the front stance, the reverse punch is executed with the arm opposite the forward leg. For example, if you enter the front stance by stepping forward with your left leg, thrust your right fist forward as soon as the stepping motion is completed.

Three important points need to be mentioned about the karate fist. First, you strike with the first two fist knuckles of the index and middle fingers. Second, make sure your thumb is secure against your rolled-up fingers and does not stick out, or it

The karate fist

might get broken. Third, hold the wrist straight, rather than bent, to prevent breaking it during a strike.

KICK

Kicking techniques are critical to all styles of karate. A kick provides added reach and strength, and keeps the heart at a distance from your opponent.

The front kick is used to attack the knee, groin, solar plexus, and chin of an opponent. From the natural stance, lift the knee in a marching style, curling the toes backward over the top of the foot. Snap or thrust the leg out and up, striking the target with the ball of the foot. Strike quickly, then return to the original position. If your leg remains extended too long, your opponent can grab it and push or pull you off balance.

The roundhouse kick relies on a rotation of the body and a snapping motion of the knee for power. It is accomplished by striking with the ball of the foot or the instep. The latter is the weaker of the two.

To kick, lift the knee waist-high, so that the foot and calf are positioned behind the body and the knee and ankle are horizontal to the floor. From head on, your legs will form a rough figure 7. Swivel your hips around so that the foot snaps out and strikes its target. Return to the chamber, also known as the figure 7 position, as soon as you strike.

Balance is key in this strike. Keep your supporting foot flat on the floor. Although your foot may rotate to help you keep your balance, avoid a full rotation. Originally facing forward, the support foot should turn about 135 degrees in the direction of the

The front kick

kick, then return to the forward position as the kicking foot returns to the chamber.

The side kick is one of the most frequently used kicks in karate. It relies on the outer edge of the foot as the striking surface. By bending the knee, bring the kicking leg into the chamber (at the knee of the supporting leg, which is also bent). Snap the leg out to the side by working the hips and slightly pivoting the supporting leg. Do not lock the kicking leg into position; instead, extend it to an almost locked position, strike, and quickly snap the leg back into the chamber. Aim at the knee, solar plexus, ribs, or face.

BLOCK

Karate defense begins with strong blocking techniques. The main idea is to deflect incoming strikes, not to stop them. The major blocks are the low, high, inside, and outside blocks, used at lightning speed to blunt your opponent's blows.

The low block is used to deflect attacks to the lower part of the body by striking with the outer edge of the arm. Stepping into the forward stance, sweep the arm from the shoulder to the opposite knee. The other arm is pulled into the chamber, providing added force to the block.

The high block protects the neck, face, and head. The idea is to lift your opponent's strike totally above your face by sweeping your arm across your body to a position slightly above your own head. Only the forearms should make contact.

*The side kick launches
from the chamber
toward its target.*

Sweeping across the body, the low block deflects an opponent's blow.

*The high block will lift
an opponent's blow overhead.*

The outside block begins with the fist of the blocking arm behind the ear on the same side. As you step forward, sweep your arm out in front of the body so that the forearm and fist face your chest and protect it by the time the block is completed.

In the inside block, the fist of the blocking arm is clenched and held underneath the opposite arm in a crossed fashion at eye level. Pull the blocking arm out and up so that the arm is bent at 90 degrees upon blocking. To protect the chest, you should bring the fist no higher than the shoulder. Lift your blocking arm higher to protect your face.

8
Green Belt

The amount of time spent at the white belt level varies. Promotional examinations may be held as often as every three months, but whether you advance to the next belt in that time, or in six months, nine months, or even longer depends on your natural ability and coordination, time you devote to training, and individual school policies. The more serious you are about developing your karate skills, the quicker you'll advance.

Once you've paid your examination fees (ranging from $30 to $50), been tested, and received your certificate of promotion, a new challenge awaits you. At the green-belt level, you will be expected to polish the skills you already possess. This means that all the techniques you learned at the white-belt level must be practiced again and again until they become instinctive and smooth. If the white-belt level is a time for introduction, the green-belt level is a time for refinement.

At the same time, new techniques will be presented to you. Kicks and strikes will be more complex. A sampling of some of the green-belt techniques follows. Though included in the green-belt section in this book, some schools present these techniques earlier and some later.

STANCE

In the side stance, you should stand with your feet parallel, about two shoulder distances apart. Squat slightly, lowering the torso toward the floor.

To move forward or backward in this position, the back leg moves toward and crosses over the front leg in a scissors motion. Once the back leg is anchored, the front leg then moves ahead again to put you back in the side stance.

This stance allows you the option of turning to face multiple opponents. To do this, follow the steps above, but instead of planting the back leg, pivot on the forward leg just as the back leg approaches it. Once your pivot is complete and you are facing the opposite side, continue the forward motion with your back leg until you are again in the side stance.

The back fighting stance is taken by stepping back with one foot. Your feet should be at 90-degree angles to each other and about one and one-half shoulder widths apart. They are firmly planted, with the toes gripping the floor. Both knees should be bent, but the bulk of your weight should be supported by the rear leg. Keep your head facing forward.

To move forward in the back stance, glide the back leg forward and ahead of the front leg. The front leg simply pivots and becomes the rear leg in a new back stance. Reverse this process to move backward.

STRIKE

The elbow can be used in multiple ways to disable an opponent. In the horizontal elbow strike, the elbow is used to attack the right

The back fighting stance

or left side of your opponent in the chest, face, and temple. Begin in the natural stance, with one hand in the chamber and the striking hand behind the opposite ear. Step into the side stance, while at the same time pushing your elbow out and around, keeping your forearm parallel to the floor. Ideally, your body should be positioned at 90 degrees to your opponent.

To strike a glass-jawed opponent, you'll want to know the vertical elbow strike. While in the natural stance, swing the elbow upward in as sharp an angle as possible to make contact with the underside of the chin. As in the horizontal elbow strike, the other hand remains in the chamber throughout the technique.

If you master the spear hand strike, you'll resemble Bruce Lee in action. In this move, the fingers are fully extended, with the thumb crooked over the palm. Begin with the striking hand in the chamber. As your target approaches, thrust out your hand and strike the ribs, solar plexus, throat, or eyes with the fingertips.

The close punch resembles a hook in boxing. From the chamber, the fist travels up toward the point under the solar plexus or the ribs, with the two front knuckles making contact. A technique for close fighting, you do not corkscrew your fist as in the thrust punch. This punch begins and ends palm up.

KICK

The crescent kick serves two purposes. It can be used offensively as a striking technique and defensively as a block. In either case, the arch of the foot is used to make contact.

The spear hand
uses the fingertips
to strike a target.

Similar to a slap in the face, only with the foot, the crescent kick is best applied when striking a target opposite the kicking foot. That is, if the target is to the left, strike with the right foot. If the target lies to the right, use the left foot.

Assuming that your target is to the left, lift your right leg and sweep it across your body toward your intended striking area. Your knee should be bent slightly as you lift your leg and strike. After hitting your target, continue the rotation so that your supporting leg turns 90 degrees to its original position. Bring the kicking foot back to the opposite knee for blocking protection and to ready yourself for your next move.

BLOCK

There will be times when one arm will not be a strong enough defense against a powerful kick. The double arm block will be a useful tool. To block with the left arm, tightly clench both fists and pull them as far back to the right side as they'll go. The right fist should jut straight back to the rear. As you begin the block, swing first your left arm and then your right arm up and across to the left side of your body. Turn your fists and forearms at the last moment to face you. The left arm will bend 90 degrees, with the fist at slightly higher than shoulder level. The right arm will reinforce the left arm by touching it at the left elbow joint. Additional blocking power comes from locking in the chest muscles.

9
Brown Belt

After studying karate for two years and possibly longer, you will be ready for the brown (or red) belt. Even if this is as far as you ever advance, it is quite an accomplishment. Only the most serious students make it to this rank.

At this level, a student's moves are expected to be more specific and defined. Where earlier you concentrated on learning the basic techniques and adding some refinement, the brown-belt student is expected to perfect the form and execution of the moves.

It is at this level that you will practice *combinations*, multiple techniques while moving. In tang soo do karate, *hyungs*, or forms, become the basis of instruction. The form enables a student to rehearse two or three basic karate techniques while moving through a series of prearranged steps. The *kata* in Japanese shotokan karate is the form's counterpart. Again, the kata is a series of prearranged steps that allow you to practice specific techniques, but the idea behind the kata is symbolic combat.

Some basic techniques you will be expected to know at this level are described on the following pages. Typically, they are not techniques that a karate student would be called on to use frequently, but having knowledge of them is critical, for it is believed that the greater a person's knowledge, the better prepared he or she is to meet life's challenges.

STANCE

Your face extends forward in the hourglass stance with the feet parallel to each other, about two shoulder widths apart. The toes of both feet turn in, and the knees are bent. With clenched fists outstretched at the side, the body resembles an hourglass.

Another stance, which is introduced earlier but perfected at this level, is the cat stance. Supporting 90 percent of your weight, the back leg is held at 45 degrees to the forward leg and is bent at the knee. The front leg rests only on the ball of the foot and is practically free of all weight so that quick strikes will be possible with that leg.

STRIKE

Green belts are powerful fighters, but their knowledge of technique is not yet controlled. Brown belts, on the other hand, are not only powerful, they're calculating, able to anticipate and outwit their opponents because they know which techniques will work best against any given rival. Introduced early in the study of karate, two techniques that brown belts practice and refine until flawless are the sacrifice and takedown.

The sacrifice is used against a heavier or stronger attacker or against someone wielding a knife. Using the element of surprise, this technique enables you to quickly stun an opponent.

Stand in the natural stance. As the attacker approaches you head on, fall to the left or right side, tucking the leg closest to the floor under you. Use the other leg to execute a roundhouse kick to your attacker's rib cage or solar plexus (see Chapter 7). If you want to strike in the face, use your arms to push your body off the floor and you'll gain the necessary height.

Before the attacker recovers from your kick, it's necessary for you to push against his knee with one leg and against his ankle with the other. With ample force, this scissoring motion will break his knee, making you the victor.

In karate there are many types of takedowns. One of the most basic is also one of the most powerful.

Beginning in natural stance, block a lunge punch with an overhead block (left hand blocking a right punch and vice versa). At the same time, step into a forward stance slightly to the outside of your opponent's body. This move to the side will enable you to grab the punching arm with your blocking hand and to pull your opponent off balance. At the same time you unbalance your rival, use the palm heel of the other hand to push against your opponent's opposite shoulder. (You pull with the blocking hand and push with the other for leverage.) Simultaneously, sweep your inside foot against the inside foot of your opponent, to unsteady that leg. After throwing your opponent to the floor, deliver the decisive blow to the solar plexus, throat, or face.

KICK

By the time you reach the brown-belt rank, your knowledge of kick techniques will be vast. One of the most dramatic and most frequently photographed is the flying side kick. To kick with the right leg, it will be forward in the side stance. Move the left leg forward and jump off it, pulling in the right knee as close to the chest as possible. As you kick, thrust out the right leg and simultaneously snap the left leg back into the body. (Remember, karate draws its power from force coupled with counterforce.) After striking your target, allow both legs to relax, and land on the balls of your feet.

Takedowns are
used to unbalance
an attacker.

One of the most powerful kicks is the ax kick. Its source of power is the momentum and weight you focus on the leg as you bring it down on your opponent. Its effectiveness lies in the difficulty your opponent will have in blocking a kick that is coming down on, rather than toward, him.

The ax kick is done from the front stance. With the left leg forward, you'll kick with the right leg. Lift the right leg straight up as high as possible. You must lock in the knee and tense the calf and thigh muscles to avoid injury to your knee. Jut the heel of the right foot forward by turning the toes and ankle up. Complete the technique by bringing the heel straight down on your opponent's collarbone.

BLOCK

An effective block in close fighting that will enable you to break an opponent's nose, collarbone, or elbow is the chicken block. In the cat stance, block the attacker's punch with the back of your wrist by bringing the blocking hand up from the waist. Keep your fingers pointed down and close together. Force your opponent's hand above your head, and then counter with a blow to his face, collarbone, or arm.

One of the most powerful kicks in karate is the ax kick.

10
Black Belt

After studying karate seriously for two and a half to three and a half years, you will have learned all the stances, strikes, kicks, and blocks that are necessary for empty-handed combat. When you have practiced them until they are as natural to you as breathing, you will become a candidate for the black belt, the highest rank attainable in gup level.

In Korean karate, there are ten *dans* (levels of expertise) at the black-belt rank. In theory, no tenth-dan masters exist because that level represents perfection and no human can achieve this. In practice, however, many individuals have ranked themselves as tenth-dan black belts for the prestige. Be aware that the tenth dan has never been awarded by any recognized promotional committee. In Japanese karate, only eight dans are authorized by the Japanese minister of education and the Federation of All Japan Karatedo Organizations. A person becomes a master when he or she reaches the fourth dan.

The black belt is the person who is frequently portrayed in movies and on television. It is the black belt who demonstrates the ability to break bricks or thick pieces of wood, something that should *not* be tried by students without their instructor's supervision. Remember, you remain a student until you reach the fourth dan of black belt.

When you become a candidate for black belt, you must learn many advanced kicks, multiple techniques, and advanced katas. All of the katas (forms) stress speed or power, for although you have the knowledge of technique, you still must learn to control your muscles, to tighten or relax them for optimum power and speed. Remember that loosening the muscles gives greater speed, while focusing or tightening them creates power. Once this concept is mastered, you'll be able to succeed against a quicker or stronger opponent.

MULTIPLE TECHNIQUES

Multiple techniques actually begin at the white-belt rank and continue throughout your training. In a typical multiple technique, you may practice a particular kick and strike together—front kick and lunge punch, for example—to become accustomed to using them together. Multiple techniques improve your coordination, balance, and muscle control—all basic to karate skill. As you advance in rank, the number of combinations you become familiar with increases, as does your skill at completing them in a fluid motion.

KATA

While the kata (form) also improves your coordination, balance, and muscle control, it is different in concept from multiple techniques. The idea behind the kata is simple: you pretend you are being attacked from all sides by a number of people. When you perform a kata, you're turning in one direction to block and strike, then turning to the other direction to block and kick. You're moving backward and forward, from side to side, in a constant defense against imagined foes. Each kata teaches you how to handle yourself against a specific number of opponents.

As with multiple techniques, the katas begin at the white belt level and continue throughout training. Before advancing in rank, the karate student must prove knowledge of the katas and skill at performing them at each level. And at each level, the katas require more advanced skills and refinement of technique.

A properly trained student will not like to fight. Besides receiving physical training, the karate student is trained to recognize the power, responsibility, and humility that accompany the black belt. The power possessed at this level can be deadly; therefore, a black belt will first attempt any alternative to actual combat. Only when all other alternatives have been exhausted will the black belt engage in fighting. And then it is with specific purpose.

11
Competition

Short of defending yourself and training in your school, competition is probably the only chance you'll have available to test your knowledge and ability of karate technique. Most karate schools hold competitions for their students. You can learn about other contests through fliers posted at most karate schools and by reading karate and martial-arts magazines. Some schools, however, require an instructor's permission to enter or observe a contest.

In self-defense karate, the object is to disable your opponent so that you are not hurt. In sport karate, you spotlight technique in a match that may last two, three, or even four minutes. The idea is to see how effectively you can pick your targets, move across space, and work technique for a hit.

Winners are usually awarded trophies. But most of all, winners gain the satisfaction of knowing they've executed the moves smoothly enough to be awarded winning points by the four to five judges. Whether you win or lose, competition should reward you with increased knowledge.

Most karate contests have several types of competitions, and people tend to specialize in one or two of them, focusing on their strengths. Competitions exist in semifree sparring, freestyle sparring, and individual or group kata.

Semifree sparring is a step up from the choreographed one-step sparring that is practiced in training halls. In this type of sparring, the "attacker" is not limited in choice of moves. The only requirement is to identify what part of the body is going to be struck. It then becomes a contest to see if the defender can *psych out* the opponent by anticipating *how* the strike will come and which countermoves will make the best defense.

Freestyle sparring is an advanced form of practice and is the closest to real combat. None of the moves is known beforehand. Each contestant is free to attack at will and to decide which techniques will score points. A point will be awarded only when a focused, controlled hit is made to a specific part of the body. This idea sets karate apart from other combative sports, like boxing. In karate, it is NOT necessary to actually hurt your opponent, only to show that you could. Therefore, the strikes are "controlled," meaning they stop just short of connection.

Whether performed individually or in a group, the kata is judged like a gymnast's routine; that is, its difficulty is weighed along with its execution. Some katas may be performed in as little as one minute, but their length is not a factor in scoring. The elements that judges look for are correctness of form, defined movement, and concentration. A short but expertly performed complex kata will win out over an awkwardly attempted kata that is less difficult and longer.

Before you enter a tournament, it is a good idea to enter something local to become familiar with the competitive scene. When you know what to expect, you're less likely to be caught off guard. Also, an often unmentioned factor in winning is behavior and personality. Judges often make assessments of contestants before they actually compete. Humility and good manners are looked on with a kinder eye than bragging and improper decorum. Entering local competition will acquaint you with behavior that is deemed acceptable before, during, or after a match.

Once you enter a tournament, become familiar with the floor by examining it beforehand and even by practicing a few techniques. A change in surface can throw a contestant off balance or cause hesitation.

You should also practice with a partner in your school before entering competition. Pacing is an important factor in karate. You need to begin and to finish with the same strength and speed. Duplicating the tournament situation in your school will help you to adjust your pacing so that your strength isn't burned up during the first few seconds of competition.

If you make a mistake during competition, don't stop. Chances are the judges didn't catch it. Or maybe it wasn't a mistake at all!

12
Modern Heroes

As in any other sport, karate has its own celebrities. But in spite of the sport's long history, its list of stars is relatively recent, dating back only to the 1960s when the popularity of sport karate became widespread.

Their names are colorful. Brooklyn's "Hawk" Frazier earned his nickname because he had a reputation for perfect flying kicks. Bill "Superfoot" Wallace was world middleweight champion during most of the 1970s. Tom "La Puppet" Caroll was the second man and the first black to be inducted into the Black Belt Hall of Fame in 1969. More recently, Steve "Nasty" Anderson received the 1986 Joe Lewis Cup, awarded to the top fighter of the year and as prized in karate as the Heisman trophy is in football.

Synonymous with karate are the names Bruce Lee, Joe Lewis, and Chuck Norris. It was the late Bruce Lee who focused attention on the sport through a series of action-packed martial-arts films with a theme of good versus evil. Lee repeatedly triumphed over the villains through a remarkable display of swift action and skill.

Lewis and Norris, on the other hand, gained recognition as

rivals in competition karate during the late 1960s. Each man had combined what he thought were the best techniques of different styles of karate so that a new style of fighting emerged. A match between the two was a real spectacle. Lewis has continued his involvement with the sport through the promotion of full-contact karate and the development of the Joe Lewis Karate Systems. Norris not only turned his championship record into a successful system of schools, but also established a busy movie career.

As the sport continues to grow, new stars are developing. Take, for instance, Martin Kove, who after fifteen years as a struggling actor has experienced "overnight" success by displaying his knowledge of karate in *Karate Kid* and *Steele Justice*.

Another *karateka* who has turned his knowledge into a money-making venture is Ernie Reyes, Jr., the fourteen-year-old star of television's *Sidekicks*. But prior to television, Reyes made karate history by becoming the youngest competitor ever to place in a national tournament—in the *adult* kata division.

13
For More Information

ORGANIZATIONS

Several organizations exist to spread knowledge of karate. Some function only in the United States; others represent members from around the world. There is probably also a local organization in your area.

National Women's Martial Arts Federation
1377 Studer Avenue
Columbus, Ohio 43206

United Martial Arts Federation
San Diego Headquarters
8967 Mira Mesa Blvd.
San Diego, California 92126

World Martial Arts Association
P.O. Box 1568
Santa Barbara, California 93102

BOOKS AND
PERIODICALS

If you want to read further about karate, the following list may be of interest.

Books

Bergarnie, Luke. *Karate.* New York: Scholastic, Inc., 1987.

Cho, Sihak Henry. *Better Karate for Boys.* New York: Dodd, Mead and Company, 1970.

Cho, Sihak Henry. *Korean Karate.* Rutland, Vermont: Charles F. Tuttle Company, 1968.

Kozuki, Russell. *Junior Karate.* New York: Sterling Publishing Co., 1971.

Reisberg, Ken. *The Martial Arts.* New York: Franklin Watts, 1979.

Sternberg, Alex, and Gary Goldstein. *From Kata to Competition: The Complete Karate Handbook.* New York: Arco Publishing, 1982.

Wilson, Jim. *Illustrated Guide to the Art of Oriental Self Defense.* London: Marshall Cavendish Publications, 1975.

Magazines

American Karate
Condor Books, Inc.
351 West 54th Street
New York, New York 10019

Black Belt
P.O. Box 7728
Burbank, California 91510

Combat Karate
Horizon Publications, Inc.
1180 Avenue of the Americas
New York, New York 10036

Inside Karate
Subscription Department
P.O. Box 404
Mt. Morris, Illinois 61054

Newsletter

Tang Soo Do News
11655 Duenda Road, Suite D
San Diego, California 92127

Karate Terms

Bunkai: (Japanese) A form of practice similar to a kata, but real rather than imaginary "attackers" are used.

Chamber: The "ready" position in which fists and feet are held before executing strikes and kicks.

Chung shim: (Korean) The body's balance point.

Combinations: A form of practice in which multiple karate techniques are combined while moving.

Dan: A degree, or level of achievement, within the rank of black belt.

Do bohk: (Korean) The karate uniform.

Dojang: (Korean) Training hall or school.

Dojo: (Japanese) Training hall or school.

Focus: The point at which you tense your muscles to maximize power.

Form: A series of moving steps in which you repeatedly practice one or two karate techniques.

Freestyle sparring: Competition fighting in which none of the moves is known beforehand. Freestyle sparring is the closest thing to real combat you'll likely encounter, short of scrapping on the street.

Gup: (Korean) The degree, or level, of achievement at ranks below black belt. This term is sometimes spelled k-u-p.

Hara: (Japanese) The body's balance point.

Hyung: (Korean) Form.

Ippon: (Japanese) This is a point awarded in competition for a focused, controlled hit.

Ja Yu Dae Ryun: (Korean) Freestyle sparring.

Je Soo Sik Dae Ryun: (Korean) One-step sparring.

Karate-gi: (Japanese) The karate uniform. It is sometimes shortened to just *gi*.

Karateka: A person who studies karate.

Kata: (Japanese) This is a dancelike movement of choreographed steps, strikes, blocks, and kicks in which the performer imagines being attacked by multiple foes.

Kiai: (Japanese) The yell that summons strength. It assists in concentrating mental and physical power on a specific target. In Korean this is called *Ki Hap*.

Ki Hap: (Korean) See **Kiai**.

Kumite: (Japanese) Freestyle sparring.

Kyu: (Japanese) The degree, or level, of achievement at ranks below black belt.

One-step sparring: A system of practice that simulates person-to-person combat, with the aggressor taking only one step forward to initiate the strike, which is known to both partners beforehand and met with a specific block. There is also three-step and five-step sparring.

Sah Bum Nim: (Korean) A karate master and instructor.

Semifree sparring: This is an advanced form of one-step sparring. Here the attacker is not limited in his strikes, but the target area must be announced before a strike is taken.

Sensei: (Japanese) A karate master and instructor.

Waza-ari: (Japanese) A half-point or almost a point awarded in competition.

Index

About the Author

Larry Dane Brimner has written *BMX Freestyle* and *Footbagging* for Franklin Watts. His writing has also been published in children's magazines. He teaches writing and other courses in the education department of San Diego State University, San Diego, California.